Helping Children See Jesus

ISBN: 978-1-933206-68-4

LAW AND FAITH
New Testament Volume 26
Galatians Part 1

Author: Marilyn P. Habecker
Illustrator: Frances H. Hertzler
Computer Graphic Artist: Ed Olson
Typesetting and Layout: Morgan Melton, Patricia Pope

© 2018 Bible Visuals International
PO Box 153, Akron, PA 17501-0153
Phone: (717) 859-1131
www.biblevisuals.org

All rights reserved. No part of this publication may be reproduced, stored in a retrieval system or transmitted in any form by any means, electronic, mechanical, photocopy, recording or otherwise, without the prior permission of the publisher, except as provided by USA copyright law.

RELATED ITEMS

To access related items (such as activities, memory verse posters and translated texts) please visit our web store at shop.biblevisuals.org and enter 1026 in the search box on the page.

FREE TEXT DOWNLOAD

To access a FREE printable copy of the teaching text (PDF format) in English or other available languages, enter S1026DL in the search box. Add the item to your cart, and use coupon code XTACSV17 at checkout. Once your order is processed you will receive an email with a link to the free download.

"We have believed in Jesus Christ, that we might be justified by the faith of Christ, and not by the works of the law."

Galatians 2:16b

© Bible Visuals International Inc

Lesson 1
SALVATION BY FAITH

NOTE TO THE TEACHER

The book of Galatians was written by the Apostle Paul for the specific purpose of declaring that people are saved entirely by grace (God's loving favor) through faith in the Lord Jesus Christ. Further, he taught that salvation cannot be had by doing good works even the good work of keeping the law.

Before the Galatian people had first heard the glorious Gospel of Christ, they were idol worshipers. When Paul preached to them, they accepted the Gospel message with enthusiasm and turned to serve the true God of heaven.

However, after Paul left them, false teachers came among them. They declared that something more than faith in Christ is required to obtain salvation. These teachers insisted that it was also necessary to keep the laws (which God had given to Moses hundreds of years before the death of Christ), including the ritual of circumcision. Only by doing these things could anyone earn salvation, these false teachers said.

The Galatians were confused. Some began to follow what the false teachers taught. When Paul heard that news he immediately wrote a letter to the Galatians. We shall be studying that letter in three parts:

Chapters 1 and 2–Personal
(Paul defends his authority as an apostle
Law and Faith

Chapters 3 and 4–Doctrinal
Paul defends the Gospel
Law and Grace

Chapters 5 and 6–Practical
Paul applies the doctrine
Law and Liberty

The study of the Galatian letter is extremely important because there is much teaching that attempts to add something to the message of salvation which is by divine grace alone. Many feel that they must earn their salvation.

Before beginning to teach this volume, it would be helpful to review NT Volume #5 *Faith*.

Scripture to be studied: Galatians 1 and 2; Acts 8:1-3; 9:1-22

The *aim* of the lesson: To help pupils understand that salvation cannot be earned by keeping the law or doing good works. Salvation is God's free gift to the one who believes in His Son.

What your students should *know*: The Word of God makes it clear that we are saved through faith in the Lord Jesus alone.

What your students should *feel*: A desire to receive God's gift of salvation.

What your students should *do*: Put their trust in the Lord Jesus Christ and receive Him as Saviour.

Lesson outline (for the teacher's and students' notebooks):

1. Paul, once an unbeliever, turned to Jesus and preached the Gospel.
2. The Galatian believers were confused by false teachers.
3. The darkness of our sin makes God's love shine more brightly.
4. Salvation is a free gift to all who will receive it.

The verse to be memorized:

We have believed in Jesus Christ, that we might be justified by the faith of Christ, and not by the works of the law. (Galatians 2:16b)

THE LESSON

1. PAUL, ONCE AN UNBELIEVER, TURNED TO JESUS AND PREACHED THE GOSPEL

Today we shall begin to study another book in the wonderful Word of God, the letter to the Galatians. It was written by the Apostle Paul.

Paul had once been an unbeliever. Even then, however, he was a very religious man. He tried to keep the ritual of the law which God had given through Moses. As religious as he was, he refused to believe that Jesus was the Son of God. He thought Jesus was a false prophet. So he would not place his trust in Him.

Show Illustration #1a

Do you remember some of the terrible things Paul did thinking he was pleasing God? (*Teacher:* Encourage the class to discuss Paul's persecution of the early believers, as recorded in Acts 7, 8 and 9.)

Show Illustration #1b

Paul was changed from being an enemy of Christians to a faithful witness concerning Christ. (*Teacher:* Let class review the events of Paul's conversion.)

After Paul believed on the Lord Jesus Christ and received Him as his own Saviour from sin, he began traveling through neighboring countries, telling the wonderful news of the Gospel. God had performed a great miracle. He had taken a man who hated the Gospel of Christ and changed him into a man who risked his life and suffered many hardships so others might hear the same good news.

Show Illustration #1c

Paul went from city to city preaching the Gospel of salvation through faith in the Lord Jesus. Many of those who heard him could hardly believe that this was the same man.

They said, "Paul is the one who used to search out Christians so that he might have them put in prison or killed. But now he himself believes in Jesus. And he is preaching the same Gospel he once tried to destroy!"

In the region of Galatia, many listened to the message which Paul preached. Many of them trusted in the Lord Jesus Christ and gave up their worship of idols. Because of their faith in Jesus Christ, God saved them and counted them righteous.

2. THE GALATIAN BELIEVERS WERE CONFUSED BY FALSE TEACHERS

Paul could not stay long in one area, however, if he was to reach all who needed to hear the Gospel. So he traveled on to other places. After leaving Galatia, Paul learned some bad news. False teachers had gone to the Galatian believers saying that people could be only partly saved through faith in the Lord Jesus Christ. They also had to obey the law which God had given hundreds of years before Christ died. They told the Galatians that by keeping the law, they could earn their salvation. But that was not true.

The false teachers preached another untruth. They said that if a person is to be *kept* saved, he/she must do good works and keep the Jewish law. Of course this was not true. When anyone receives the free gift of salvation, the Holy Spirit comes to dwell in that person and keeps him/her saved. It is God who saves and keeps him/her saved. A person's good works do not save or keep him/her saved. (However, after a person is saved, he/she naturally wants to and will do good works.)

The Galatians were confused. When Paul was with them, they seemed to understand perfectly that they were sinners for whom Christ had died, and that they had received God's free gift of salvation. Now that these other teachers had come, they wondered, *Can these men be right and Paul wrong?*

Show Illustration #2a

Has that sort of thing ever happened to you? Let us suppose that you have decided to visit the home of a friend. But you are not sure how to get there. A man comes along, and you ask him, "Could you tell me how to find Juan's house?" (*Teacher*: Use a name familiar to your group.)

The man answers, "Oh, you go that way. His house is down that way." (Point to left, *teacher*.)

As you walk along, you begin to feel a bit uncertain. *Was that man right?* Just then you see another man and you decide to ask him for help.

"Sir, could you tell me how to find Juan's house?"

Show Illustration #2b

"Yes. He lives up that way." (*Teacher:* point to right this time.)

Now you are really confused. Two men have given you directions, but they do not agree. So you know one of them has to be wrong. But which one?

This was probably how the Galatians felt. Paul had taught them one thing. The new teachers were preaching something else. Which was right?

If Juan himself came along while you were searching for his house, could you trust his directions? Why? (*Teacher:* Allow class to respond.) Because Juan lives there, he knows the right way.

Sometimes we may feel like the Galatians. One person tells us the way to receive God's gift of salvation is by placing our trust in the Lord Jesus. Someone else may say, "That is not enough. You must do certain other things to earn salvation." Which one will we believe? Whose word will we accept? Can you think of Someone who really knows the answer, One whose word is always true and right?

Yes, God knows the right answer and His Word is always true. His Word says that a person is not declared to be in right standing with God by obeying laws, but by trusting in Christ. If we could be in right standing with God by keeping laws, then Christ died for nothing. (See Galatians 2:16, 21.)

3. THE DARKNESS OF OUR SIN MAKES GOD'S LOVE SHINE MORE BRIGHTLY

Did Christ die for nothing? Certainly not!

But if a person could be declared right by keeping laws, Christ would not have needed to die. Could people really keep the law perfectly? Let us look at some of the laws God gave. (*Teacher:* Study Exodus 20:1–24:12. Pick out laws that apply to your particular group and discuss them. For example, if any in your group have worshiped idols, read Exodus 20:4. Have all in your class always kept God's day holy? (See 20:8-11). Have they always honored their father and mother? (See 20:12.) Did anyone ever steal? (20:15.) Or tell lies? (See 20:16.) Discuss several commands to show that no one has ever kept the entire law.)

Perhaps you're thinking, *There are many, many laws.* (You are right, for there are more than 600 altogether.) But, you think, *I have broken only one law. To break only one out of so many cannot be so wrong. God would not hold me for that!*

Let's suppose that this rope which I hold in my hand represents God's laws. (*Teacher:* You may prefer to use a chain or a fishing net–whichever is best for your people.) It looks like a good rope. Suppose the rope is holding a goat. If the rope breaks in just one place, would the goat get away? (If only a part of the net was broken, would the fish get away?) Of course. Even if only one part of the rope broke, the entire rope is broken. So it is with God's Law. If a person breaks only one law, the whole Law is broken because he has sinned against God who gave all the Law. (See James 2:10.)

None of us has kept the whole Law. Why, then, did God give the Law if He knew that no one could keep it? He gave it so that we would realize what sin is. (See Romans 3:19-23.) If we didn't know what God's Law is, we wouldn't know that we are sinners. (See Romans 7:7.) It is the Law that helps us to understand how holy God is. And it is the Law that shows us that we all have come short of His perfect standard of righteousness. (See Romans 3:23.)

We would like to forget our sinfulness because it makes us ashamed. But the darkness of our own sinful selves makes God's love and mercy shine more brightly.

Show Illustration #3

When you look up at the sky on a clear night, you see how bright and beautiful the stars are against the darkness of the sky. Have you ever seen the stars shining in the daytime? No? Yet they are shining. The reason you cannot see them is because it is light. The darkness of the night sky shows off the sparkling beauty of the stars. So it is with God's love. When we understand how sinful we are, we appreciate His love much more.

4. SALVATION IS A FREE GIFT TO ALL WHO WILL RECEIVE IT

Because we are sinners, none of us could ever keep the law of God. One Person alone, the Lord Jesus Christ, obeyed God's law perfectly (1 Peter 2:21-23). The perfect One took all our sins and the punishment for them upon Himself and died in our place (1 Peter 2:24). Only by believing in Him can we have forgiveness of sin and eternal life. We cannot earn salvation, no matter how many good works we may do or how many laws we may keep.

Show Illustration #4

God's salvation is a free gift. It is a gift made possible by God Himself who gave His Son to die for us.

Have you placed all your trust in the Lord Jesus alone? Do you understand that you are a sinner and that He died and rose again for you? Have you received God's free gift of salvation? Or have you been confused, like the Galatians, thinking that you have to do something good in order to earn salvation and have your sins forgiven? Remember, the Word of God can be believed. And God's Word says that it is only through faith in the Lord Jesus that we're saved. (See Ephesians 2:8-9; Titus 3:5.) Will you put your trust in Him today?

Lesson 2
SALVATION IS NOT BY WORKS

NOTE TO THE TEACHER

You will remember that the theme of Galatians is this: salvation is by God's grace through faith in Christ, in contrast to the false teaching that salvation is by the good works which we do. In Lesson #1, we introduced Paul as the author of the letter and presented the circumstances surrounding the writing of the letter. In this lesson we will use the experiences of Cain and Abel to illustrate the difference between faith and works. Although this part of the lesson appears in Genesis, remind your pupils that we are studying truths taught in Galatians. Remember that review is imperative.

Cain is a perfect example of a typical natural man. He is religious and believes in God. But he rejects God's way of salvation and attempts to please God through his own merits. God never saves a person because of his/her good deeds. God saves a person because he/she believes in the Gospel of Jesus Christ. What is included in the Gospel? We are all sinners. God put all our sin on Christ. By dying on the cross, He took all the punishment for all our sin. He rose again, proving that God accepted His sacrifice. Make this clear to your students. (See Isaiah 53:6; 1 Corinthians 15:3, 4.)

Scripture to be studied: Galatians 1, 2; Genesis 4:1-17; Hebrews 11:4; 1 John 3:12

The *aim* of the lesson: To show that no matter how good or right our works may seem to be, they are not acceptable to God. We cannot work for our salvation. We must come to God His way: through faith in His Son, Jesus Christ.

What your students should *know*: There is only one way to God: we must place our trust in the Lord Jesus who took the death punishment for our sin.

What your students should *feel*: A desire to place their trust in the Lord Jesus.

What your students should *do*: Believe in the Lord Jesus Christ and receive him as Saviour.

Lesson outline (for the teacher's and students' notebooks):
1. Forgiveness of sin comes through shedding of blood.
2. God accepts a sacrifice of blood.
3. God knows every wrong that is done and will forgive those who turn to Him.
4. God punishes those who will not turn to Christ.

The verse to be memorized:

We have believed in Jesus Christ, that we might be justified by the faith of Christ, and not by the works of the law. (Galatians 2:16b)

REVIEW

1. Who wrote the letter to the Galatians? (*Paul*)
2. Why did Paul write this letter? (*False teachers had gone among the Galatians, preaching that having faith in the Lord Jesus Christ was not sufficient to save them. They said that in addition, people had to obey the law and do certain good works.*)
3. What did Paul teach the Galatians in this letter? (*Faith in the shed blood of the Lord Jesus is the only requirement for salvation.*)

THE LESSON

Paul was amazed. He couldn't believe that the Galatians, who had received the Gospel eagerly, could turn away to a teaching that was untrue. False teachers had added some of their own ideas to the Gospel of Christ. Paul wanted the Galatians to believe only what God's Word said–not what men taught. He said, "Even if I, myself, came to you and preached a message different from the true Gospel of God, you should not believe it. If an angel from Heaven preached a false gospel, let him be accursed [doomed]." It is a serious thing to mislead others regarding their relationship to God.

The story is told of a woman who was taking a long trip by bus during the rainy season. She had her tiny baby with her, and she was worried because the rain and wind blew fiercely. She was afraid that she might get off the bus at the wrong place; so she asked the driver to help her.

"Of course," he said. "I will tell you when we come to the right place."

A man sitting nearby overheard what she said and told the woman, "I travel this way often. I will be glad to help you. The driver will probably forget."

Before long, the bus stopped and the man said, "The driver forgot, just as I thought he would. But this is the right place." So the woman stepped out into the storm, trying to protect her baby.

A bit later the driver stopped and called for the woman. When he learned what had happened, he exclaimed, "You made a mistake! She may die in the storm."

He turned back to search for her, but it was too late. Both the woman and her baby had been caught in a swollen river and drowned. The man had given her wrong information. So she and her baby were dead.

That was a terrible thing to do. But it is even worse to give wrong information which may cost a person eternal life or rob him/her of a lifetime of joy and peace which he/she could have by trusting in the Lord Jesus.

Paul reminded the Galatians, "If salvation comes by keeping the law, instead of by faith, then Jesus died for nothing. His sacrifice was of no use." Paul wanted the Galatian believers–and us–to remember this truth from God's Word: In order to be saved, God does not ask for good works. He asks for genuine heartfelt belief in Christ.

1. FORGIVENESS OF SIN COMES THROUGH SHEDDING OF BLOOD

Show Illustration #5

When the first man and woman, Adam and Eve, obeyed Satan, they became sinful and were no longer fit to walk and talk with God.

God had made them for Himself. So He killed an animal and used its skin to make coverings for them. He was showing them that there is no forgiveness of sin without the shedding of blood. (See Hebrews 9:22.) From that time on, they could approach God only by offering a blood sacrifice for their sins.

Time passed and two sons were born to Adam and Eve. The first, Cain, grew up to be a farmer. Abel, the second son, became a shepherd. They probably watched their father offer sacrifices to God. When they asked him about the meaning of the offerings, they learned how awful sin is and how loving God is.

Their father must have told them about their former beautiful home which he and their mother once had in the garden of Eden. "There were many lovely plants and trees in the garden. There was plenty of food for us–delicious food. There was only one tree of which God said we were not to eat. We had enough food without that tree. But one day Satan tempted us to eat that fruit. And we chose to obey him. That evening we did not want to meet God as we had always done. So we hid among the trees. When God found us, He told us that we would have to leave the garden. Because we had disobeyed God, we deserved to die. But God killed an animal and used its skin to make coverings for our bodies. He killed the animal instead of us because He loved us. Ever since that day, whenever we bring an offering to the Lord, we bring an animal. Its blood is a covering for our sin." The boys understood this.

2. GOD ACCEPTS A SACRIFICE OF BLOOD

Cain and Abel grew to manhood, old enough to bring their own sacrifices to God.

Show Illustration #6

Abel built an altar and placed wood on it. Then he carefully chose his best lamb–a perfect one. He killed it, cut its throat and poured out its blood. Then he placed it on the altar and confessed his sins to God. God was pleased with Abel and his offering, and He accepted his sacrifice.

Cain built his altar. But he decided he would offer a different kind of sacrifice. He had something more beautiful to give than a dead lamb. Cain gathered fruits and vegetables–things which he had grown with his own hands. He piled them on his altar. There was no shed blood in his offering. There was nothing to remind him of how much God hates sin. His offering didn't make him remember that something else had to take the punishment for his sin. There was none of that. Cain thought only of the beautiful things on his altar.

He waited for God to show that his offering was accepted. But God wasn't pleased with Cain's offering. He refused to accept it. Cain, instead of being ashamed, was angry, and his face showed his bitterness.

"Why are you angry?" God asked Cain. "If you bring the right offering, it will be accepted. You know I will forgive your sin if you obey Me. There is, even now, a lamb lying at the door of your tent. If you refuse to bring it, sin lies at the door of your heart."

Did Cain get the lamb and offer it? No, he didn't. He turned away from God. He chose his own way rather than God's way.

3. GOD KNOWS EVERY WRONG THAT IS DONE AND WILL FORGIVE THOSE WHO TURN TO HIM

The hate in Cain's heart grew. He was angry with God, and he was jealous of his brother Abel. He was so angry, so jealous, that he killed his brother. (The first person born into this world was a murderer!) Then Cain hid Abel's body.

Show Illustration #7

In a little while the Lord God called to Cain, saying, "Where is your brother Abel?" Because God sees and knows all things, He knew what had happened. But He was giving Cain the opportunity to confess the sinful thing he had done.

Cain would not repent. He had disobeyed God in not bringing a blood offering. He had been angry with God. And he had killed his brother because of hatred and jealousy.

Cain answered God with a lie, "I don't know where my brother is. He's not my responsibility."

"Cain, what have you done?" the Lord demanded. "I know that you killed your brother. And because you have done this, the ground will never again give its best for you. You will be a wanderer over all the earth."

4. GOD PUNISHES THOSE WHO WILL NOT TURN TO CHRIST

Show Illustration #8

For the rest of his life Cain wandered from place to place, always getting farther away from God.

Poor, foolish, sinful Cain! Do you know anyone like him? God offers His free gift of salvation to all people everywhere. All He asks is that they believe in His Son who died to take the punishment for their sin. But many, instead of accepting God's way, offer Him something else. They prefer their own way, doing things they think are good, rather than trusting in God's Son.

God must punish that kind of person, no matter how many good things he has done. That punishment is everlasting death– separation forever from Him and from all that is good.

Abel obeyed God and offered a blood sacrifice to take the punishment for his sin. God accepted Abel and his sacrifice.

The way to God has always been the same: by faith through blood sacrifice. Faith is believing in God's Son; believing that we are sinners who cannot save ourselves; believing that God loves us and gave His Son to take the death punishment for our sin; believing that the Lord Jesus proved He is the Son of God by rising from the dead. The only way to be saved is by believing in Him and receiving Him as Saviour. This is to have faith in Him. And faith is just the opposite of working to earn our salvation. Abel came to God by faith, Paul came to God by faith, and you can come to Him by faith, too.

Paul had taught the Galatians the way of faith. He had to speak harshly to them when they were deceived by the false teachers. Do not let yourself be deceived. A person is declared right, not by doing the works of the law, but by faith in Jesus Christ. (See Galatians 2:16.)

If you have never placed your trust in Him, will you do so right now?

Lesson 3
PAUL WAS REALLY AN APOSTLE

NOTE TO THE TEACHER

The ministry of Paul and Barnabas in the province of Galatia on their first missionary journey is recorded in Acts 13:14–14:23. At Antioch in Pisidia Paul preached that the Lord Jesus was the Saviour whom God had promised (Acts 13:23).

He added that the Law of Moses could not justify anyone. Christ offers complete justification to every believer (Acts 13:38-39). Many people heard the Word of God (v. 44), and some believed in the Saviour (v. 48). This made many of the Jews jealous, and they drove Paul and Barnabas out of town.

The missionaries went to another town in Galatia, Iconium (14:1-5). There a great multitude believed the Gospel (14:1). When Paul and Barnabas learned that the unbelievers planned to stone them, they fled to Lystra. They preached the Gospel there (14:7,) and Paul miraculously healed a man who had been lame from birth. This so astonished the people that they believed the missionaries were gods and prepared to make sacrifices to them (14:11-13). Paul immediately corrected them, saying that they were to turn to the living and only true God (14:14-18). Shortly afterwards the same people who had thought the missionaries were gods stoned Paul, dragged him from the city and left him for dead. But God did a miracle and raised him. The next day Paul and Barnabas went to Derbe and preached the Gospel in that city (14:20-21).

They revisited these cities in Galatia. They taught the new Christians, who apparently were suffering persecution, that we must endure tribulations before entering God's kingdom (14:22). After appointing elders in the new churches, they commended them to the Lord (14:23). This was the beginning of the work in Galatia. Paul wrote the Galatian letter to these people.

Scripture to be studied: Galatians 1, 2; and all the references in the lesson.

The *aim* of the lesson: To point out that Paul was really an apostle chosen by God. Because he was truly God's messenger, we can believe his message of salvation by faith in Christ, plus nothing.

What your students should *know*: Paul's message of salvation for everyone is by trusting in Jesus Christ alone and not through works.

What your students should *feel*: A desire to believe in the Lord Jesus.

What your students should *do*: Believe that Jesus Christ is God's Son, that He died for them and receive Him as Saviour.

Lesson outline (for the teacher's and students' notebooks):
1. God calls Paul and teaches him about Himself.
2. Paul is accepted as an apostle.
3. Paul becomes the apostle to the Gentiles.
4. Paul rebukes Peter for obeying Jewish laws.

The verse to be memorized:

We have believed in Jesus Christ, that we might be justified by the faith of Christ, and not by the works of the law. (Galatians 2:16b)

REVIEW QUESTIONS

1. What is the Apostle Paul telling the Galatians in the beginning of his letter to them? (*Salvation is through faith alone and not through faith plus works.*)
2. How do the sacrifices of Cain and Abel illustrate the difference between works and faith? (*Allow the class to discuss the previous lesson.*)
3. What does our memory verse tell us about salvation through faith? (*Lead the class in reviewing Galatians 2:16b. Discuss it briefly.*)

THE LESSON

There is another Scripture passage that is very much like our memory verse. It says, "For by grace are you saved, through faith; and that not of yourselves: it is the gift of God, not of works, lest any man should boast" (Ephesians 2:8-9).

Salvation is a free gift from God and cannot be earned in any way. Does this mean, then, that Christians should not try to do good deeds? No! They want to obey and serve the Lord to show their love for Him and to demonstrate their faith to others. God wants their loving service after they have been born again. But they do not become God's children by doing good works.

Were the Galatians proving their love for God by doing good works? No. They were trying to make certain that they really were children of God. This they did by performing old Jewish ceremonies and by keeping old Jewish laws. They were attempting to earn their salvation. Poor, foolish Galatians!

1. GOD CALLS PAUL AND TEACHES HIM ABOUT HIMSELF

Why do you suppose the Galatians doubted the truth of what Paul had taught them and accepted the teaching of false teachers? Apparently they weren't certain that Paul was really an apostle chosen by God to preach the Gospel. Because of that, Paul used the first two chapters of Galatians (about one-third of the entire book!) to tell five things that happened which proved that he was indeed an apostle and that his message was true. Suppose we let Paul himself tell what happened.

"Brothers in Christ, I guarantee that the Good News which I preached to you did not come from a man. The Lord Jesus Christ revealed it to me. You remember what kind of a life I lived before I met Jesus. I opposed the Christian believers so violently that some were sent to prison and others were put to death. (See Acts 9:13-14; 26:10-11.) I knew more about our Jewish religion than many Jews my age. I was eager to follow the traditions of our Jewish fathers. But God had other plans for me.

Show Illustration #9a

"One day along the Damascus road, I saw the risen Christ and He spoke to me. I knew He was the Lord (Acts 9:6) and immediately gave myself to Him. That changed my whole life. Instead of hating Christians, I was one of them. But I didn't talk with anyone at the mother church in Jerusalem about my call from God. I tell you, I am an apostle because God Himself called me to be His messenger.

Show Illustration #9b

"After God called me, I went to the desert of Arabia and was alone with Him. During that time He taught me the truths of the Gospel which I have preached to you. Just as the first twelve apostles were taught by our Lord during their years of being with Him, I was taught by Him during the time I was alone with God.

2. PAUL IS ACCEPTED AS AN APOSTLE

Show Illustration #10

"Three years after I was saved I went to Jerusalem and spent fifteen days with Peter. (See Galatians 1:18-20.) I wanted to get to know him and the other apostles. (See Acts 9:26-29.) Like them, I had seen the risen Lord. (See Acts 9:27; 1 Corinthians 9:1; compare Acts 1:22.) But I didn't need to be taught by them because God Himself had taught me. He had already used me as His messenger in Damascus. The apostles who were there at that time accepted me as an apostle. In Jerusalem I preached boldly about the Lord Jesus, so boldly that some of the Greek-speaking Jews plotted to murder me. Throughout the province of Judea the Christians praised God for the Gospel. I preached the same Gospel that your false teachers say is not sufficient.

3. PAUL BECOMES THE APOSTLE TO THE GENTILES

Show Illustration #11

"After serving the Lord for 14 years, God commanded me to go again to Jerusalem. (See Acts 15:1-29; Galatians 2:1-10.) This time I was to talk with the church leaders about the message I was preaching throughout the area where Gentiles live. (The church leaders had been preaching primarily in the region where the Jews live.) Barnabas, my fellow missionary, and Titus went with me to Jerusalem. Even though Titus was an uncircumcised Gentile Christian, the church leaders did not command him to obey the Jewish ritual (circumcision). If that was necessary in order to be saved, as the false teachers have taught you, certainly these church leaders would have insisted on Titus's obeying that ritual. At the meeting of the whole church which followed, some false brethren came in like spies, trying to find out whether or not we obeyed the Jewish laws.

"They wanted us to be bound by their rules, like slaves in chains. We refused to listen to them, for we didn't want anyone to be confused, thinking that salvation can be earned by following Jewish ritual and obeying Jewish laws." (*Teacher:* Use illustation to point out that Christ's cross is all important. The old Jewish laws, written on tablets of stone, are crossed out, done away with.)

"James, our Lord's brother (the head of the Jerusalem church), and Peter and John, two of the leaders, understood that I had been made an apostle to the Gentile region just as Peter was an apostle to the Jewish region. They realized that God had used me just as He had used Peter. These great leaders gave Barnabas and me the right hand of fellowship, accepting us as brother apostles. Would they have done this if I hadn't been called of God as an apostle? Certainly not!

4. PAUL REBUKES PETER FOR OBEYING JEWISH LAWS

"Another thing happened which proves that I am a true apostle called of God. (See Galatians 2:1-21.) Once when Peter visited Antioch in Syria, he ate and had wonderful times with Gentile Christians who do not follow Jewish ritual or obey Jewish laws.

"Then some Jewish Christians–claiming to be friends of James–came to Antioch. Because Peter was afraid of what they would say about Jews and Gentiles eating together, he refused to eat with the Gentiles any more. All the other Jewish Christians, even Barnabas, followed Peter's example. By doing this, they were really saying that the people who had been saved by Christ needed something more: they needed to follow Jewish ritual and obey Jewish laws.

Show Illustration #12

"So all the people would know that Peter was wrong in what he had done, I rebuked him in public, saying, 'You and I are Jewish Christians. We know perfectly well that we didn't become right with God by obeying Jewish laws. The law was such a perfect standard that no one could ever keep it entirely. So instead of saving us, the law condemned us. It was by faith in Christ alone that we were declared right by God.' This was what I said to Peter that day in Antioch. Peter did not and could not answer me because he was wrong. God kept me true to His Word. You Galatians can know that I am truly an apostle appointed by God."

Someone might tell you that he/she does not believe a person can be saved by faith in Christ alone. When you answer him that the Apostle Paul taught that truth, the person might say, "How do you know that Paul was really an apostle?" You could tell him/her the five things that we have learned today. You should list these in your notebook:

Paul Proved He was an Apostle
Galatians 1:10-2:21

1. On the Damascus road, Paul saw the risen Lord. At that time he was called to be God's messenger, an apostle.
2. God Himself taught Paul when he was alone with Him.
3. After three years Paul went to Jerusalem. The apostles who were there at that time accepted him as an apostle.
4. Fourteen years after his conversion, Paul went again to Jerusalem and was given the right hand of fellowship as an apostle to the Gentiles. He was accepted by all the other apostles.
5. At Antioch, when Peter refused to eat with Gentiles, Paul rebuked him openly. If Paul had not truly been an apostle, Peter would have refused to listen to him.

Paul was indeed an apostle called by God. The message he gives is directly from God. What is his message? It is this: God saves us when our trust is in His Son alone. We are not saved by the works of the law. Do you believe this?

If you have never placed your trust in the Son of God, will you do so right now? God loves you, even though you have sinned. Because you are a sinner, Christ died for you. He took your punishment. God accepted His death for you and to prove it, Christ rose from the dead. Now He waits for you to receive Him. Will you do that now?

Lesson 4
FAITH

Scripture to be studied: Galatians 1 and 2; Matthew 7:24-29; Luke 6:47-49

The *aim* of the lesson: To help your students understand the necessity of receiving Christ by faith and encouraging them to witness to their friends so they may have the privilege of leading them to Him.

What your students should *know*: Without faith in the Lord Jesus, it is impossible to be saved.

What your students should *feel*: A desire to share their faith.

What your students should *do*: Tell someone this week how they can put their trust in the Lord Jesus and be saved. Write in their notebooks the names of those to whom they want to witness this week.

Lesson outline (for the teacher's and students' notebooks):

1. To be saved, a person must hear the Gospel.
2. To be saved, a person must look to the Lord Jesus.
3. To be saved, a person must believe the Gospel message.
4. To be saved, a person must believe in the Lord Jesus and receive Him as Saviour.

The verse to be memorized:

We have believed in Jesus Christ, that we might be justified by the faith of Christ, and not by the works of the law. (Galatians 2:16b)

REVIEW QUESTIONS

1. Why was the book of Galatians written? (*Allow class to restate the circumstances surrounding the writing of Galatians, as presented in the first lesson. Remember, the Galatians were believers in Christ; they had received salvation by faith. Their error was that later they were disturbed by false teachers who argued that works were essential to salvation in addition to faith in Christ.*)
2. Why did God accept Abel's offering, but reject the offering of Cain? (*Be sure that the class understands that God shows no partiality, for God is not a respecter of persons. God shows no partiality today in saving some and condemning others. It is up to each individual either to choose God's way or to reject it.*)
3. How do we know that Paul was really an apostle? (*(1) He had seen the risen Lord on the Damascus road and was called to be God's messenger, an apostle. (2) He spent time alone with God, and God taught him. (3) When he went to Jerusalem, the apostles who were there accepted him as an apostle. (4) After fourteen years, Paul went again to Jerusalem and was accepted as an apostle by all the apostles. (5) Paul rebuked Peter publicly at Antioch, and Peter accepted the rebuke.*)
4. What was Paul's message to the Galatians (and us)? (*Salvation is by faith alone in the Lord Jesus Christ, plus nothing.*)

NOTE TO THE TEACHER

The Bible has given us a description of faith in Hebrews 11:1: "Faith is the substance of things hoped for, the evi-dence of things not seen." That is, faith is being certain we will get what we hope for and being sure of things we cannot see. Faith is the foundation stone upon which we base our salvation–as opposed to the sandy foundation of works.

For a more complete study of faith–what it is, how it operates, its source and its results–refer to New Testament Volume 5. If you have already taught that volume, a brief review would be in order. If you have not taught that volume, you may want to teach those lessons before proceeding with more lessons in Galatians.

THE LESSON

We have been learning that it is through faith only that we are saved. Faith is believing God and taking Him at His word. To have faith is more than to know in your mind what the Gospel is; it is to trust the Lord Jesus deep down in your heart as God's Son and your Saviour from sin.

If you are now a child of God you are probably concerned for your family and friends who do not know Christ as Saviour. That is good. You should have a great desire for them to come to Him. You know and understand that they must have faith in Him alone. But how are they going to have that saving faith? There are four things that form part of a person's having faith in Christ.

1. TO BE SAVED, A PERSON MUST HEAR THE GOSPEL

Show Illustration #13

First, your friend must hear the Gospel. The Bible says, "Faith comes by hearing." (See Romans 10:17.) The Old Testament prophet Isaiah said, "Hear, and your soul shall live" (Isaiah 55:3). How can your friend's soul live? He must hear the Gospel message. Is he ready to listen to you? Has your own life been so changed that your friend wants to hear about salvation?

When you tell the Gospel to others, are you making it perfectly clear that there is no way to be saved except by faith in Christ alone? The Galatians became confused because the false teachers taught that it was necessary to obey certain laws in order to be saved. Make no mistake when you tell the Gospel to others. Don't add anything to the clear teaching of the Word of God.

2. TO BE SAVED A PERSON MUST LOOK TO THE LORD JESUS

If your friend is going to have faith in the Lord Jesus, he/she must hear the Gospel and must look to the Lord Jesus. God says in His Word, "Look unto Me, and be ye saved…for I am God, and there is none else" (Isaiah 45:22). Jesus Himself said, "I am the way, the truth, and the life: no man cometh unto the Father, but by Me" (John 14:6).

Show Illustration #14

Your friend cannot see the Lord Jesus with physical eyes. But if he/she is to have saving faith in the Saviour, your friend must turn the eyes of his/her heart and mind to the Lord. The risen, living Lord Jesus wants to bring him/her to God. (See 1 Peter 3:18.) Help your friend to turn his/her attention to the Lord Jesus, Who is the originator and perfecter of faith. (See Hebrews 12:2.) He is able to save completely those who come to God by Him. He prays that they will do just that. (See Hebrews 7:25.) There is no way to come to God for salvation except through faith in the Lord Jesus Christ. Good works will not save anyone. Obeying rules and laws will not result in salvation. Being born into a Christian family does not mean that a person is saved. Help your friend look to Jesus.

3. TO BE SAVED A PERSON MUST BELIEVE THE GOSPEL MESSAGE

If your friend is to have saving faith, he/she must hear the Gospel, look to the Lord Jesus, and believe the Gospel message.

What is the Gospel message? Christ died, taking the punishment for our sins, He was buried and proved He is the Son of God by rising again the third day according to the Scriptures. (See 1 Corinthians 15:3-4.) Your friend must believe this with all his/her heart. Only by believing in the Lord Jesus can he/she have eternal life. (See John 3:15-18.) To believe means to trust. We must take God at His Word. Believing in the Lord Jesus is to trust that He will save us forever.

The Lord Jesus told a story that shows what happens when people hear the Gospel. The story was about two men who built houses.

Show Illustration #15a

One man, Jesus said, dug deep and built the foundation of his house on a rock. The other man did not build a foundation for his house. He simply built it on the soft, shifting sand.

Both houses were probably beautiful, made of the finest materials. Then a great storm came. The winds howled and drove the rain and floodwaters against the houses with terrible force. The raging flood pounded away against the walls of the two houses.

Show Illustration #15b

The storm beat vehemently against the house on the rock, but did not even shake it. The same storm beat just as furiously against the house on the sand. Immediately it fell, completely destroyed.

Jesus said that the person who hears Him and believes what He says, is like the wise man who built on the good foundation. The person who hears the Gospel and does not believe it, Jesus said, is like the foolish man who built on the sand. A person who places his/her trust in his good works, in church or in anything else, however good, is building on sand. Invite your friend to build on the Lord Jesus alone. Encourage him/her to place his/her faith in Christ, who is the solid Rock. (See 1 Corinthians 3:11.)

4. TO BE SAVED ONE MUST BELIEVE IN THE LORD JESUS AND RECEIVE HIM AS SAVIOUR

To be saved, your friend must hear the Gospel, must look to the Lord Jesus and must believe that He is who He says He is–the Son of God. One other thing is included if a person is to have saving faith. He/she must receive the Lord Jesus Christ as his/her own Saviour from sin. He/she must place his/her trust in Him. God's Word says, "As many as received Him, to them gave He power to become the sons of God, even to them that believe on His name" (John 1:12).

Your friend may listen to the Gospel when you tell it to him/her. He/she may have his/her attention turned to the Lord Jesus. He/she may even say that he/she believes what you have said about Jesus. But the person cannot become a child of God until he/she places his/her complete trust in Him.

Suppose you come to a foot bridge high above a raging river. You look at it and say, "I believe it can hold me so I can cross to the other side." You could repeat it all day long: "I believe the bridge can hold me." Still you stand there looking at it. Do you truly believe that the bridge will hold you? No, you don't. You only say you believe it. You prove that you believe it will hold you by stepping on it and walking across. That is faith.

Genuine faith in the Lord Jesus includes believing in Him and receiving Him. God has made His way of salvation available to your friend (and to all people everywhere). But your friend cannot be saved until he/she receives Christ.

Let's suppose we live in a valley where all the crops are dying because of a drought. On top of the hill is a large lake. There is plenty of water in the lake but it cannot get out. Is the lake water of any use to the dry ground below? No. What could we do? (*Teacher:* let your pupils discuss the possibilities.)

Show Illustration #16

We could get a huge bamboo. (*Teacher*: If bamboo is unknown to your students, use pipe instead. You may want to change the picture to make it look like a pipe.) Let us call our bamboo *Faith*. We can place one end of the bamboo in the lake and direct the other end to the valley below. Soon a rushing stream of water will flow down and the crops will be saved.

This is how faith works. All the promises of God and the saving power of God are available. God's way is the only way of salvation. What must your friend do in order to be saved? He/she must use faith. By saying, "I believe in the Lord Jesus Christ and receive Him as my Saviour," and meaning what he says, your friend will be using faith. Then salvation will be his/hers.

Remember! Your friend must HEAR the Gospel. What is the Gospel? We all are sinners. But Christ took the punishment we deserve when He died on the cross. Because God accepted Christ's sacrifice, He rose from the dead and lives. Your friend must LOOK to Jesus for salvation. He/she must BELIEVE that Jesus is the Son of God. He/she must RECEIVE Him as his/her own Saviour from sin. This is genuine saving faith. And it does not include doing good works. (See Ephesians 2:8-9; Titus 3:5.)

The Bible says that "without faith, it is impossible to please God" (Hebrews 11:6). This week will you invite your friend to place his/her complete trust in Jesus Christ?

www.ingramcontent.com/pod-product-compliance
Lightning Source LLC
Chambersburg PA
CBHW060804090426
42736CB00002B/154